boat

open

letter

boy

Some words in the English language are used much more frequently than others. Three hundred words make up three quarters of all that we speak, read or write. These have been called Key Words. This book illustrates one hundred of these most used words.

Acknowledgments:
READ with me! Key Words to Reading is written by William Murray with stories by Jill Corby.

British Library Cataloguing in Publication Data

Picture dictionary.
    1. English language. *Readers*
    I. Series
    428.6
    ISBN 0-7214-1416-8

First edition

Published by Ladybird Books Ltd Loughborough Leicestershire UK
Ladybird Books Inc Auburn Maine 04210 USA

Printed in England

READ with me!

Picture Dictionary

cat

fish

illustrated by ANNE MATTHEWS

Ladybird Books

apple

baby

bag

ball

bed

bird

black

blue

boat

book

box

boy

bus

cake

car

cat

chair

children

cow

cup

Dad

DANGER

dog

doll

door

down

draw

eat

drink

egg

farm

fire

fish

first

5
five

flower

4 four

girl

green

hand

hat

head

hill

horse

house

jam

jump

last

letter

man

men

milk

money

Mum

night

no

one

open

over

pen

pencil

picture

play

Police

pull

push

rabbit

rain

read

red

road

room

run

school

sea

seat

shop

sing

street

sun

sweets

table

tea

television

3 three

toy

train

tree

2 two

under

up

van

water

white

window

woman

women

write

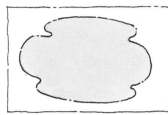

yellow

ZOO

List of words in this dictionary

apple

baby
bag
ball
bed
bird
black
blue
boat
book
box
boy
bus

cake
car
cat
chair

children
cow
cup

Dad
DANGER
dog
doll
door
down
draw
drink

eat
egg

farm
fire
first
fish

five
flower
four

girl
green

hand
hat
head
hill
horse
house

jam
jump

last
letter

man
men